T0082634

DISCOVER YOURSELF!

A Practical Guide for Teenage Young People to Identify, Outline, and Live Their Unique Purpose!

JUNE CLARE BUGENYI

authorHOUSE

AuthorHouse™ UK
1663 Liberty Drive
Bloomington, IN 47403 USA
www.authorhouse.co.uk
Phone: 0800.197.4150

© 2018 June Clare Bugenyi. All rights reserved.

No part of this book may be reproduced, stored in a retrieval system, or transmitted
by any means without the written permission of the author.

Published by AuthorHouse 02/22/2018

ISBN: 978-1-5462-8403-1 (sc)
ISBN: 978-1-5462-8814-5 (e)

Print available on the last page.

Any people depicted in stock imagery provided by Thinkstock are models,
and such images are being used for illustrative purposes only.
Certain stock imagery © Thinkstock.

This book is printed on acid-free paper.

Because of the dynamic nature of the Internet, any web addresses or links contained in this book may have changed
since publication and may no longer be valid. The views expressed in this work are solely those of the author and do
not necessarily reflect the views of the publisher, and the publisher hereby disclaims any responsibility for them.

Contents

Discover Yourself!

Scripture quotations marked "KJV" are taken from the King James Version of the Bible.

Scripture quotations marked "MSG" are from THE MESSAGE. Copyright © by Eugene H. Peterson 1993, 1994, 1995, 1996, 2000, 2001, 2002. Used by permission of NavPress Publishing Group.

Scripture quotations designated (NIV) are taken from the Holy Bible: New International Version®. NIV®. Copyright © 1973, 1978, 1984 by International Bible Society. Used by permission of Zondervan. All rights reserved.

Scripture quotations marked "NKJV" are taken from the New King James Version. Copyright © 1982 by Thomas Nelson, Inc. Used by permission. All rights reserved.

To all the young people whose hopes appear to be dashed.
You are God's masterpiece. He is waiting for you!

Acknowledgements

This work is a result of combined efforts from different individuals and institutions who through their time, knowledge, experience and interest in the development of others, have strengthened the desire in my heart to write this guide.

I am forever grateful to God Almighty, my Father, my Saviour and Friend who saw me through, from the birth of the idea until the production. His grace has been sufficient and brought helpers to uplift me when discouragement tried to creep in

To my teachers Professor Vincent Anigbogu and Dr Sunday Adelaja whose teachings opened my eyes and challenged me to desire living a fulfilled life of transforming other peoples' lives.

To my Publishing Consultant, Harry Zayne from Author House. You have been a blessing from the time I mentioned of the idea; you have encouraged and guided me through the process which appeared a great mountain before me but you broke it down for me to climb it.

To the Editorial and Design teams from Author House, thank you for looking through the document and your help into designing the layout and cover design; personally I wouldn't have done it any better.

To youngsters Peace Tembo and Joshua Olaleye, the first young people I tested this guide on. You availed yourselves to be taught through this guide while on its raw stages an experience which restored confidence in what I had desire to achieve. The lessons I learnt from working with you helped me improve the guide.

To my Lifespring Church and the Africa Christian Fellowship families. You allowed me serve in the Junior Church and Director for Youth and Talent Development respectively, an opportunity that strengthened my passion to see the lives of young people transformed.

To my friend Marina Abraham. You have been a great source of encouragement and an advisor from the time we learnt we have the same passion of seeing the lives of young people transformed.

To my siblings, you have encouraged me to go for what I believed in something which at times denied you the opportunity of my fellowship when you most needed me

What others have to say about this guide

This guide is a must-have for every young person who wants to discover his or her purpose. The book's step-by-step guidance makes it easy to be used by individuals, as a group, and by teachers and parents alike. I highly recommend it!

—Joshua Olaleye, student, Bath University, UK; and Vice President, Africa Christian Fellowship, UK

The preparation provided to the student is awesome! For me, this guide achieves many things! It will help develop a truly grounded Christian child! Even if one were to stop at that, this guide is still an investment. It equips the student or the trainee. It is a teaching, and an altar call. This piece of work exposes the user to the ministry of evangelisation and then to the ministry of coaching.

—Joyce Murigi, parent and entrepreneur, Nairobi, Kenya

I found this to be an uplifting, inspirational book about living with true Christian purpose. In it, the author shows readers, both young and old, that we do indeed have important reasons to live.

—Editor, AuthorHouse, UK and USA

Background

It was not until after November 2010, when I underwent a training in Ukraine known as History Makers' Training, that I started wondering what my purpose was here on earth. Am I living because I get up in the morning and I have not died as have many who went to sleep and never got up? Am I living because God has not yet decided to take my breath away? Am I living to work, get paid, one day get married, have children, and raise them until they too get married? What comes next? I die. *Is that all?*

I came to realise that if that is all, then all I have been pursuing is *vanity*!

But wait a minute ... I know that God is not a waster of time and resources. Life might be in vain if, after the fall of humankind, God had not sent His Son Jesus to redeem creation (both humankind and the earth). Jesus set the pace of redemption; He gave His disciples of His time and of this generation a prototype of the process of redemption. This is why He said, "Most assuredly, I say to you, he who believes in Me, the works that I do he will do also; and greater works than these he will do because I go to My Father" (John 14:12 NKJV).

Now the questions that followed me from the training were: June, why are you still alive? What is your purpose here on earth? With such questions in mind, I started reading and/or listening to teachings and materials related to life purpose and realised that I have a purpose here on earth; I am not just here by chance. God has put within me unique attributes that are key and necessary to the continuation of the process of redemption that Jesus Christ started over two thousand years ago. I came to realise that God has preserved me to this day, has given me as a covenant to the people, to restore the earth and cause the people to reassign their desolate heritages (a reference from Isaiah 49:7–8). In me there are solutions for the ongoing challenges of the society to which I belong.

With that understanding, I began to find out what the purpose is for my life. I did this by taking myself through a process of identifying the areas that *I desired to see change*—a change that would reflect God's values and principles.

I came to the realisation that I am a change agent, just as Jesus said:

> You are the salt of the earth; but if the salt loses its flavour, how shall it be seasoned? It is then good for nothing but to be thrown out and trampled underfoot by men. You are the light of the world. A city that is set on a hill cannot be hidden. Nor do they light a lamp and put it under a basket, but on a lampstand, and it gives light to all who are in the house. Let your light so shine before men, that they may see your good works and glorify your Father in Heaven. (Matthew 5:13–16 NKJV)

So if this is what I am, I am expected to shine, not for my own glory, but for the glory of the one who created me, ensuring that His values and principles are sown into society.

God is giving us another opportunity to discover and understand our role as believers in the societies we are part of. My role is different from yours, and no role is greater or better than any other. As Paul said, "But now indeed there are many members yet one body. And the eye cannot say to the hand, 'I have no need of you,' nor again the head to the feet, 'I have no need of you.' No, much rather, those members of the body which seem to be weaker are necessary" (1 Corinthians 12:20–22 NKJV).

Personally, I am still in the process of fully discovering who am I by seeking to understand the *mind of God concerning my life*, and working on myself to realise my full potential. In the meantime, with that which God has helped me to know, I cannot wait to share it with the body of Christ so that we will all get into the process of discovering who we are and live to realise our purpose.

This guide is not the ultimate, but it does set the pace and lay out the process whereby individuals, using the principles detailed herein, together with real-life experiences, can come up with a personal approach to living the life God has predestined for each one of them.

Jesus cautioned us, saying, "I am the true vine, and My Father is the vinedresser. Every branch in Me that does not bear fruit He takes away; and every branch that bears fruit He prunes, that it may bear more fruit" (John 15:1–2 NKJV).

As we embark on the journey of discovering and fulfilling our life purpose, it is my prayer that we will one day hear the voice telling us, "Well done, good and faithful servant; you were faithful over a few things, I will make you ruler over many things. Enter into the joy of your lord" (Matthew 25:21 NKJV).

God bless you!

Introduction

The majority of adults today are not sure of what they are living for. There are those who are living the dream of their parents, who made them pursue careers that the latter thought were prestigious and would bring honour to the family. Others are pursuing careers because of the success they have seen other people achieve in those careers. Others are pursuing a line of work because of the financial gain involved. The majority fall in the category of those just doing what was available at the time. Very few people are doing what they are passionate about, what they enjoy doing.

The same trend trickles down to our young people. They have very little, if any, guidance to help them make life-transforming decisions. The majority of them have fixed their eyes on the music and entertainment industry or a career in sports because they believe these jobs are quick to obtain and are very profitable, both materially and socially (the latter in terms of fame). The majority of our young people do not see themselves as future adults who will have a responsibility for shaping the destiny of the society and world they live in. Many of them do not imagine that one day they will become individuals who will be expected to implement important decisions that will have a direct impact on the lives of others, including their own immediate family members and others around them. Our young people have not been taught to think of the future. What a tragedy! It is sad to see some senior adults still taking full responsibility for the lives of their young adults; the young adults still depend fully on their parents or guardians. In some societies, where the parents are not in a position to be there for their young adults, the responsibility has become that of the Social Services Department where they are provided with basic needs such as food and shelter. In a long term the young adults are 'denied' the opportunity to grow into mature men and women to take responsibility for their own lives and society. What will end being of such a nation in say twenty years' time? How long can this be allowed to continue? But again, we ask ourselves, what can the seniors do? Because they themselves were never taught that they carry the solutions to the ongoing societal challenges, they cannot give what they do not have.

On top of this, many people seem to blame the younger generation for the ongoing ills of society; we consider them as irresponsible, rude, stiff-necked, and unwilling to learn or listen, among other things. In the midst of all the blame we cast upon them, we forget to ask ourselves very important questions: How much have we invested in them? How well have we instilled in them a sense of self-value? We should not wait to invest in them until they start getting involved in crimes, at which point we begin creating or offering rehabilitation programmes. How many do we positively affect with those programmes? Probably not as many as have strayed!

It is high time we break this chain and start investing in the lives of our young people while they are still in our hands. The first thing we need to make them understand is the fact that each of them is unique, and that not every one of them is born to be a footballer, a singer, an actress, etc. Each one of them needs to find that unique nature within them. Once it is found, it needs to be nurtured, watered, and allowed to grow into an attribute that will bring meaning to the lives of other people. *Yes, we must make our young people know that they can transform society through their passions, gifts, and talents,* and that they can do it in their own different ways.

I believe that this training guide will allow us to bring out the unique gifts, passions, and talents that our young people do not even realise they possess. By using this guide, we can assist them in living a focused life that not only is meaningful to young people but also is a solution to many of the social challenges in their midst.

Let us always remember that *when there is no destination to look forward to, people do not get anywhere!*

Overall objective

The overall objective of this training guide is to practically facilitate our young people who are believers and followers of Jesus Christ to:

- ❖ Identify their passions and purpose in life.
- ❖ Devise a strategy and systems to realise their passions and life purpose, with room for growth. As they grow older, they will come to

understand that they are continuing the work of redemption which was started by Jesus Christ.

Overall outcomes

All the young people who will be trained by the suggestions in this guide are expected to:

❖ Understand that they are transformers of society who carry solutions required by the society they live in and/or represent.
❖ Identify a particular challenge within a particular sphere of society to which they believe their attributes, gifts, and talents will bring a sustainable solution.
❖ Draw a blueprint of what they want to achieve in their lifetime, detailing the goals they wish to achieve and strategies they will implement to realise those goals.
❖ Learn to take responsibility for their personal lives by spending time and resources on that what adds value to their overall life purpose.

Method of assessment

The main method of assessment will be the use of *individual tasks* which will either be completed during the session or taken home for consideration and/or a deeper analysis. Though the guiding questions used are the same, the responses are expected to be unique, suited to the passion and life purpose of the individual assessed.

The assessments will be progressively spread throughout the different sessions and will be discussed for further input.

By the end of the training, everyone is expected to have a vision statement complemented with long-term, midterm, and short-term goals.

Timing of Sessions

The facilitator will determine the timing of sessions depending on the age groups he or she will be working with. Some groups might require a slower pace compared to the other. However, the sessions should not be 'rushed' and on the other hand not 'dragged' as the young people might lose interest

Section 1

The beginning of our Christian faith

Preliminary notes to the facilitator(s)

The Christian faith is founded on the victorious work of Jesus Christ done on the cross. We understand from the Bible that God's original plan for humankind was hampered when Adam fell into the sin of disobedience. However, with God's plan being unchanging, He sent His only begotten Son to redeem both humankind and the earth, both of which were lost after the fall of humankind.

It is therefore very important for every believer to understand the meaning of Jesus's death on the cross and resurrection from the dead. Such understanding is fundamental to establishing the choices we make in life as God's instruments of expanding His kingdom here on earth.

This section is meant to lay out the foundation of our Christian faith to young people. By the end of the section, our young people will be able to understand that whatever they desire in life ought to be a means to advance the kingdom of God and not merely a means to satisfy their personal needs or build their reputation, fame, or wealth.

Learning objectives

- ❖ To understand the creation of humankind.
- ❖ To understand God's responsibility to humankind.
- ❖ To understand the concept of the fall of humankind.
- ❖ To understand what the crucifixion, death, and resurrection of Jesus accomplished.
- ❖ To understand the concept of personal purpose.

1.1 Preliminary personal survey

Materials required

- ❖ Holy Bible
- ❖ printed questionnaires
- ❖ pens

Instructions to the facilitator(s)

- ❖ In all that our young people get involved in, they should have a personal relationship with their Creator. This is the greatest miracle that can happen in their lives.
- ❖ During the first session, provide the young people with a questionnaire. This will enable the facilitators to understand what stage the young people are at, as far as their relationship with God is concerned.

Questionnaire

1. What does it mean to be a Christian?

    _____

    _____

2. Are you a born-again Christian? (Tick the answer applicable to you.)
    Yes   No

3. Do you know people who are born-again Christians?
    Yes   No

4. If you answered yes to question 2, do you remember praying the prayer of salvation?
    Yes   No

5. If you are born again, what motivated you to become born again? (Tick the answer applicable to you.)

    • My parents are Christians.
    • My friend convinced me.
    • Somebody kept on preaching to me and I decided just to do it for his or her sake.
    • I sincerely wanted to do it.
    • Other reason. (Mention it.) _____

6. Do you pray?
    6a) Always
    6b) Sometimes
    6c) Not at all

7. If you chose option 6c, why do you not pray?

    _____

    _____

8. If you chose option 6a or 6b, what do you pray about?

_____

_____

9. Do you attend Sunday school or youth class in your church?

    Yes   No

10.   What topics do you like to be taught in Sunday school or youth class?

_____

_____

1.2 The creation of humankind and God's responsibility to humankind

Learning outcome

In this section, the intention is for the young people to understand that God created us human beings and took the responsibility to ensure that all that we need in life is provided.

Materials required

- ❖ Holy Bible
- ❖ pens
- ❖ printed handouts—scenario 1
- ❖ printed handouts—important points to remember

Instructions to the facilitator(s)

- ❖ Depending on the number of young people in the class, divide them into groups of no more than three.
- ❖ Once the young people are settled in their groups, distribute the scenario 1 handout to the group members.
- ❖ Allow the group members to read this scenario.
- ❖ Allow the group members to share their understanding of the scenario for fifteen minutes.
- ❖ After the general discussion, ask one person to read Genesis 1:26–31.
- ❖ After the reading is finished, elaborate on the scripture while relating it to scenario 1.
- ❖ Conclude the topic.
- ❖ Give every young person a copy of the scenario and the important points to remember

Scenario 1

There was a man who was well educated and who became an accountant. He secured a very good job with a very good bank in the country of Eden.

His position provided him with the following privileges:

- a free company house
- a company vehicle with fuel provided
- school fees for up to four children, up to the university level
- a paid holiday of thirty working days per year.

Scripture reading

Then God said, "Let Us make man in Our image, according to Our likeness; let them have dominion over the fish of the sea, over the birds of the air, and over the cattle, over all the earth and over every creeping thing that creeps on the earth." So God created man in His own image; in the image of God He created him; male and female He created them. Then God blessed them, and God said to them, "Be fruitful and multiply; fill the earth and subdue it; have dominion over the fish of the sea, over the birds of the air, and over every living thing that moves on the earth." And God said, "See, I have given you every herb that yields seed which is on the face of all the earth, and every tree whose fruit yields seed; to you it shall be for food. Also, to every beast of the earth, to every bird of the air, and to everything that creeps on the earth, in which there is life, I have given every green herb for food"; and it was so. Then God saw everything that He had made, and indeed it was very good. So the evening and the morning were the sixth day.

Genesis 1:26–31 NKJV

Important points to remember

❖ When God created humankind, all He saw was good.

❖ Every human being is created in the image and likeness of God.

❖ By image, it means we have the character of God in us. This means we are loving, caring, forgiving, faithful, respectful, etc.

❖ By likeness, it means we can function like Him. This means we have the nature to create things, and that we are organised, we keep time, we give our best to all we do, etc.

❖ Before God created humankind, He had made sure that all that human beings required to live a successful and fruitful life was provided for.

❖ God blessed human beings and gave them dominion over everything He had created, including all the animals. (It is amazing that in the beginning, human beings were not afraid of animals. Instead, they had authority over them.)

1.3   The fall of humankind and the outcome

Learning outcome

In this section, the young people will come to understand the consequences of the sin of Adam and Eve and to relate these consequences to today's ongoing social challenges.

Materials required

- ❖ Holy Bible
- ❖ flip chart paper
- ❖ marker pens
- ❖ printed handouts—scenario 2
- ❖ printed handouts—important points to remember

Instructions to the facilitator(s)

- ❖ Depending on the number of young people in the class, divide them into groups of no more than three.
- ❖ Once the young people are settled in their groups, distribute the scenario 2 handout to the group members.
- ❖ Allow the group members to read the scenario.
- ❖ Allow the group members to share their understanding of the scenario for fifteen minutes.
- ❖ After the general discussion, ask one person to read Genesis 2:15–17 and another to read Genesis 3:17–19.
- ❖ After the readings are finished, elaborate on the scriptures while relating them to scenario 2.
- ❖ Conclude the topic.
- ❖ Give every young person a copy of the scenario and the important points to remember

Scenario 2

His role exposed him to huge amounts of money. One time, he was tempted and stole £40,000, thinking nobody would know. Unfortunately, that very evening, the board of trustees conducted an unexpected audit and found out that there was some money missing. This man was dismissed immediately after the investigation.

Take time to discuss the following questions:

1. Why do you think the man stole the money?
2. Why did the board of trustees decide to dismiss him immediately, without considering the amount of experience and knowledge he had?
3. Who was affected by his dismissal? Explain why.

Facilitator to explain to the young people that there are moments in life when we find ourselves tempted to do wrong things. Sometimes we think that no one is watching us but we need to remember that God sees us all. Let the young people know there are consequences for our actions

Scritpture reading

Then the Lord God took the man and put him in the Garden of Eden to tend and keep it. And the Lord God commanded the man, saying, "Of every tree of the garden you may freely eat; but of the tree of the knowledge of good and evil you shall not eat, for in the day that you eat of it you shall surely die."

Genesis 2:15–17 NKJV

Then to Adam He said, "Because you have heeded to the voice of your wife, and have eaten from the tree of which I commanded you saying 'You shall not eat of it,' cursed is the ground for your sake. In toil you shall eat of it all the days of your life. Both thorns and thistles it shall bring forth for you. And you shall eat the herb of the field. In the sweat of your face you shall eat bread till you return to the ground for out of it you were taken; for dust you are and to dust you shall return."

Genesis 3:17–19 NKJV

Important points to remember

- When God put Adam in the garden, He told him not to eat of the fruit of the Tree of Life, saying that the day he would eat of it, he would surely die. We all know that Adam and Eve ate the fruit.
- When we disobey God, there are always consequences that follow.
- After Adam and Eve ate the fruit, God's glory left them and they discovered that they were naked. This also meant that the ability to rule over every creature on earth left them.
- From that time, human beings realised that they were naked. This meant that the glory of God had left them and they had therefore become exposed. They felt embarrassed/ashamed in front of each other.
- Sin disconnects us from God. If we are not connected to God, it is very easy for the Devil to attack us.
- God said to Adam, "Cursed is the ground for your sake."
- From that moment, the ground lost its glory and strange things started appearing on earth. The ground started growing thorns and thistles, things which had not been there in the beginning.
- Thorns and thistles are the things that make human life a struggle; up until today, they cause the life of humankind to be in bondage.
- Thorns can appear in different places; they can appear at the individual level, the family level, the societal level, or even the national level.
- In the world today, thorns appear in different forms, such as rebellion, anger, malice, jealousy, disrespect, corruption, prostitution, sexual immorality, family break-up, dishonesty, civil wars, crimes, relativism, and sicknesses/diseases. These and any other forms or manifestations of sin do not please God.

> **Allow the young people to think of things they can liken as thorns and thistles in their lives, families, community and nation.**

1.4   God's plan for the redemption of humankind

Learning outcome

The main outcome for this section is enable the young people to understand that even though Adam and Eve fell into sin, God still loved them as before. For that reason, He had to send His only begotten Son to earth to deliver every person from sin.

This means that even if we today fall into temptation, we can run to God and ask for His forgiveness and He will accept us back, because *God is love* and He is *forgiving*.

Materials required

- ❖ Holy Bible
- ❖ flip chart paper
- ❖ marker pens
- ❖ printed handouts—scenario 3
- ❖ printed handouts—important points to remember

Instructions to the facilitator(s)

- ❖ Depending on the number of young people in the class, divide them into groups of no more than three.
- ❖ Once the young people are settled into their groups, distribute the scenario 2 handout to the group members.
- ❖ Allow the group members to read the scenario.
- ❖ Allow the group members to share their understanding of the scenario for fifteen minutes.
- ❖ After the general discussion, ask one person to read the Bible scripture Genesis 2:15–17 and another to read Genesis 3:17–19.
- ❖ After the reading is finished, elaborate on the scriptures while relating them to scenario 2.
- ❖ Conclude the topic by explaining the important points to remember
- ❖ Give every young person a copy of the scenario and the important points to remember

Scenario 3

For the poor managing director, life was not as it used to be. First he was withdrawn from the Association of Accountants. Then he had to vacate the company house immediately. Next, his children were withdrawn from the private school they were attending because he could not afford the fees. Also, he had to start using public transport and sometimes walking to different places because he no longer had a company car. Life became unbearable.

Having been out of job for a while, he found that things became very tough. One day he thought to himself, *What if I write a letter of apology to the Association, express how deeply sorry I am, acknowledge my mistake, and outline to them how I propose to work on myself so that I will not fall into the same trap again?*

And indeed, this is what he did. The Association decided to give him a second chance. This time he had to ensure that he worked to the best of his ability. He even planned on educating other employees on the signs of temptation.

The man was back on track, and every day he constantly reminded himself that he was not immune to temptation. Having that constantly in his mind made him more alert to signs of temptation.

1. What was the *turning point* for the accountant?

2. Do you think the Association made the right decision in allowing him back to work? Why?
3. What do you think kept the man from falling into temptation again? Why?

After the sin of Adam and Eve, God still wanted to be friends with His people. But He needed people to acknowledge their sins before He would forgive and become friends with them again.

Scripture readings

Now it happened in the process of time that the king of Egypt died. Then the children of Israel groaned because of the bondage, *and they cried out*; and their cry came up to God because of the bondage. So, God heard their groaning, and God remembered His covenant with Abraham, with Isaac and with Jacob. And God looked upon the children of Israel, and God acknowledged them.

Exodus 2:23–25 NKJV (emphasis added)

Now Moses was tending the flock of Jethro his father-in-law, the priest of Midian. And he led the flock to the back of the desert, and came to Horeb, the mountain of God. And the Angel of the Lord appeared to him in a flame of fire from the mist of a bush. … And the Lord said: "I have surely seen the oppression of My people who are in Egypt, and have heard their cry because of their taskmasters, for I know their sorrows. So I have come down to deliver them out of the hand of the Egyptians, and to bring them up from that land to a good and large land, to a land flowing with milk and honey, to a place of the Canaanites and the Hittites and the Amorites and the Perizzites and the Hivites and Jebusites. … *Come now, therefore and I will send you to Pharaoh that you may bring My people, the children of Israel out of Egypt.*"

Exodus 3:1–11 NKJV (emphasis added)

Important points to remember

- Sin always makes life hard.
- This is because God does not like to hang around where there is sin; and if God is not around, things are not good.
- For a very long time, people continued to sin, and they did not ask God for any forgiveness.
- This made them to continue to suffer.
- One time the children of Israel, thinking that they could no longer continue as they had been doing, *cried out to God*.
- God heard their cry and sent Moses to bring them out of oppression.
- Even in today's world, when we make mistakes, we can ask God for His forgiveness.
- God is forgiving and does not want any of us to suffer because of sin.
- When we ask Him for forgiveness, He is willing to forgive us. Once He forgives us, He makes us feel like we never sinned in the first place.

1.5 The crucifixion of Jesus on the cross

Learning outcome

It is expected that by the end of this session, the young people will be able to understand what Jesus accomplished by dying on the cross. Not only that, but also, because He rose from the dead, they will be able to understand what His resurrection means to us who believe. They will also be able to understand how we as children of God can partake of the blessings of the death and resurrection of our Lord Jesus Christ. It is within this section that the young people will be given the opportunity to commit their lives to Jesus. Our children are not too young to accept Jesus as their Lord and Saviour. They will be made aware that accepting Jesus into one's life is something one has to decide on his or her own.

Materials required

- ❖ Holy Bible
- ❖ flip chart paper
- ❖ marker pens
- ❖ 2 plastic crowns of thorns
- ❖ a rod
- ❖ a purple robe
- ❖ printed handouts—important points to remember
- ❖ a certificate of salvation

1.5.1 Our salvation is in Christ Jesus

Instructions to the facilitator(s)

- ❖ Ask the young people to open their Bibles and read the scriptures John 3:16 and 1 Peter 1:18–21.
- ❖ Allow the young people to share their understanding of the scriptures they have read.
- ❖ Give the young people who have not yet committed their lives to Jesus an opportunity to do so.
    - – Assist every young person individually.
    - – Take time to explain what it means to give one's life to Jesus.
    - – Let them know what sin is and that in heaven, there is no sin. However, try to avoid saying things such as "You will die and go to hell" and "You are a sinner," as they can sound condemning.
    - – Do not compel the young people to recite the prayer of salvation if you think they are not ready; provide them with time as you continue to explain things to them.
    - – For those in the group who appear ready, encourage them to recite a prayer of salvation, first by asking them to pray with their own words. You can guide them as needed.
- ❖ Conclude the topic by explaining the important points to remember allowing the young people to ask questions
- ❖ Give every young person a copy of the important points to remember

Scripture readings

> For God so loved the world that He gave His only begotten Son, that whoever believes in Him should not perish but have everlasting life.
>
> John 3:16 NKJV
>
> Your life is a journey you must travel with a deep consciousness of God. It cost God plenty to get you out of that dead-end, empty-headed life you grew up in. He paid with Christ's sacred blood, you know. He died like an unblemished, sacrificial lamb. And this was no afterthought. Even though it has only lately—at the end of the ages—become public knowledge, God always knew he was going to do this for you. It's because of this sacrificed Messiah, whom God then raised from the dead and glorified, that you trust God, that you know you have a future in God.
>
> 1 Peter 1:18–20 MSG

Important points to remember

- At the right time God sent His Son Jesus to die for the salvation of all of humankind.
- Jesus carried all our sins.
- When He was hung on the cross, all our sins were hung there with Him.
- By accepting to die on the cross, He paid the price of sin on our behalf.
- For us to have the forgiveness of our sins, first we must repent of our sins; we must want to be forgiven.
- After we have been forgiven, we need to allow Jesus Christ to come into our lives. (Read John 3:3 again.)
- When He lives in us, He helps us to cease doing the wrong things.

1.5.2 What happened when Jesus was being crucified

Instructions to the facilitator(s)

- ❖ Ask the young people to open their Bibles and read the scripture Genesis 3:17–18.
- ❖ Choose one young person (a boy) and ask him to sit on a chair at the front of the room.
- ❖ Choose three more young people.
- ❖ As the scripture Matthew 27:28–29 is being read, have the three who have been selected act out what is being read (putting the purple robe on the body and the crown of thorns on the head of the one sitting on the chair, and also giving him the reed to hold in his hand, and then bowing to him on their knees).
- ❖ After acting out the scripture, facilitator to explain the significance of all the actions that were being acted.
- ❖ Give every young person a copy of the important points to remember

Scripture readings

Then to Adam He said, "Because you have heeded to the voice of your wife, and have eaten from the tree of which I commanded you saying 'You shall not eat of it,' cursed is the ground for your sake. In toil you shall eat of it all the days of your life. Both thorns and thistles it shall bring forth for you. And you shall eat the herb of the field."

Genesis 3:17–18 NKJV

When they had twisted a *crown of thorns, they put it on His head,* and *a reed in His right hand.* And they *bowed the knee* before Him and mocked Him, saying, "Hail, King of the Jews!" Then they *spat on Him,* and took the reed and struck Him on the head. And when they had mocked Him, they took the robe off Him, *put His own clothes on Him,* and led Him away to be crucified.

Matthew 27:29–31 NKJV (emphasis added)

Important points to remember

- From the foregoing scripture, we see that God lost His friendship with Adam and Eve.
- Also, the ground was cursed and started to bring out thorns.
- God's losing His friends meant that Adam and Eve could no longer talk to God directly; they became very afraid of God and hid themselves.
- But because Jesus accepted to die on the cross for us, God regained His friends, and hope for a good life was given back to the earth.
- By the placing of the *crown of thorns* upon the head of Jesus, God's glory was restored on the earth. This means that we can overcome challenges through prayer.
- A reed is a sign of authority. When Jesus was *given the reed*, it meant that the authority that Adam and Eve lost to the satan in the garden was given back. So if we have Jesus in our hearts, we too have authority over sin and the things that God does not like
- When Jesus was *spat*, He was taking all the shame of our lives. Therefore, no one should ever make us feel that we are not of value.
- *Returning Jesus's clothes to Him* means that the original state of humanity was restored—the original Adam before he sinned.
- Because we have been saved by Jesus, He expects us to live like Him and to help other people come to know Him so that the world becomes the place which He created it to be.
- We can do this through the gifts, talents, and abilities He has given us.

1.5.3   Maintaining my salvation

Instructions to the facilitator(s)

❖ This is a follow-up session for the young people who have just given their lives to Jesus Christ.
❖ Share with them the following points.

Important points to remember

- When we accept Jesus into our lives, all He wants from us is friendship. He wants us to be His friends.
- If we are His friends, we will always want to know what He wants.
- If we are His friends, we will always want to do what He wants.
- We will know what He wants by reading His Word.
- We will also know what He wants when we pray, because in prayer we receive good ideas which we did not have before.
- From His Word, we receive instructions on how to be good people and how not to sin against Him.
- If we notice that we have done something wrong, He wants us to repent straightaway.
- When we repent, we tell Him that we are sorry for what we have done and we request that He help us not to do it again.

1.6   Why did God save us?

Learning outcome

By the end of this session, the young people will have an understanding that each one of us is called to excel (rule) in a certain aspect of life. They will understand that the reason God saved us is so that we may help other people by using the gifts, talents, and abilities He has given us. Each one of us has something that we are very good at, an area we do not struggle much in. This is essential for the young people to understand.

Materials required

- ❖ Holy Bible
- ❖ flip chart paper
- ❖ marker pens
- ❖ printed handouts—important points to remember

Instructions to the facilitator(s)

- ❖ Guide the young people to get involved in the game described on the next page.
- ❖ After the game, let the young people open their Bibles and read the scriptures Exodus 3:8, Deuteronomy 7:1–2, and Numbers 33:50–56.
- ❖ After the scripture reading, let the young people share their experiences and try to relate the game they played to the scriptures they just read.
- ❖ Conclude the topic by explaining the important points to remember allowing the young people to ask questions
- ❖ Give every young person a copy of the important points to remember

Short game

> Divide the young people into two groups, A and B.
>
> Have group A imitate young people who are busy with their phones or books, or listening to music, while in their little circle.
>
> Then group B sees them and decides that they want to take what group A has.
>
> Group A will not give up easily; they will have to fight to protect their belongings, they defend themselves.
>
> Group B will not give up; they will fight until they get everything from group A.

Scripture readings

So I have come down to deliver them out of the hand of the Egyptians, and to bring them up from that land to a good and large land, *to a land flowing with milk and honey, to a place of the Canaanites and the Hittites and the Amorites and the Perizzites and the Hivites and Jebusites.*

Exodus 3:8 NKJV (emphasis added)

When the Lord your God brings you into the land which you go to possess, and has cast out many nations before you, *the Hittites and the Girgashites and the Amorites and the Canaanites and the Perizzites and the Hivites and the Jebusites, seven nations greater and mightier than you,* and when the Lord your God delivers them over to you, you shall conquer them and utterly destroy them. You shall make no covenant with them nor show mercy to them.

Deuteronomy 7:1–2 NKJV (emphasis added)

Now the Lord spoke to Moses in the plains of Moab by the Jordan, across from Jericho, saying, "Speak to the children of Israel, and say to them: 'When you have crossed the Jordan into the land of Canaan, then you shall drive out all the inhabitants of the land from before you, destroy all their engraved stones, destroy all their molded images, and demolish all their high places; you shall dispossess the inhabitants of the land and dwell in it, for I have given you the land to possess. … But if you do not drive out the inhabitants of the land from before you, then it shall be that those whom you let remain shall be irritants in your eyes and thorns in your sides, and they shall harass you in the land where you dwell. Moreover it shall be that I will do to you as I thought to do to them.'"

Numbers 33:50–56 NKJV (emphasis added)

Important points to remember

- The reason we are believers in Jesus Christ is so that we can do His will here on earth.
- When we do the will of God here on earth, life becomes enjoyable.
- We will enjoy this life once we identify what we are very good at or passionate about.
- When we do the things we are good or passionate about, we have great joy within.
- However, life is normally not straightforward. There will be times when we will have to put in a lot of effort to get what we want.
- Some of the things we are good at or passionate about are used by other people in a very wrong or bad way, which does not please God. For example, there is music which is not good before God. There are some people who design clothes that are not very good. There are some leaders in the government who are not good. We see families are breaking up, we see people doing drugs, some people are homeless, and so forth.
- God has put in each one of us at least one thing we can do to make the wrong things right again; those things can be called areas of influence or areas of passion. For example, for people who are good or passionate about music, they can start producing good music which God likes. There might be people who would like to become leaders in the government. There might be those who are good at and passionate about fashion; they might design very beautiful and decent clothes. There may be people who do not want to see young people getting into drugs; other people who would like to feed the homeless; and people who do many other good things.
- Doing these good works might not be very smooth, but what will be pushing us to do them is the passion we have. But most importantly, we will do these things because we love God and we want to do what He asks us to do.
- We need to remember that if we do not do something about the problems of the world, those problems will start affecting us in one way or the other. For example, if we do not address the drug problem, then drug addicts might become thieves, stealing from other people. If someone does not work to help families, we might eventually see a lot of children

without parents. If someone does not write some good music to praise God, people will be listening to nothing but bad music.

- This means that each one of us needs to know what are we going to do to make this world a better place.

Question to think about:
What are you good at, or what are you passionate about, and why?

1.7 My area of passion

Learning outcome

By the end of this session, the young people will have an idea of the areas they might be passionate about and/or would like to influence and positively change. Our young people are *not* too young to start finding out their passions and purpose in life.

Materials required

- ❖ flip chart paper
- ❖ marker pens
- ❖ printed handouts—important points to remember

1.7.1 What is my passion?

Instructions to the facilitator(s)

- ❖ Start the session by asking each of the young people what they think they might want to become in life.
- ❖ After the discussion, explain the important point to remember to the young people.

Important points to remember

- Each one of has been given a specific ability, passion, or gift.
- God expects us to use that ability, passion, or gift to make Him known to others.
- If we are children of God and we use our gifts, passions, and abilities properly, many people will start to know what God wants for this world.
- When we go to church, we are taught God's truth about our lives so that we may become better people during the week when we are with people who are not of our faith.
- As we become better each day, we make God known, because people will always want to be like us. They will listen to us because they will see that we are giving them solutions to their problems.
- The sooner we discover our area of influence, the greater impact we will have in our community.
- Age is not a factor. Even young people have done great things to influence the world. (The facilitator can give practical examples of young people who are making an impact in their areas of influence.)

1.7.2 Why should I know my passion?

Instructions to the facilitator(s)

- ❖ Start the session by splitting the young people into groups to discuss the following quotation of Lucius Annaeus Seneca.
- ❖ Conclude the topic by explaining the important points to remember allowing the young people to ask questions
- ❖ Give every young person a copy of the important points to remember

Quotation for discussion

> When a man does not know what harbour he is
> making for, no wind is the right wind.
>
> —Lucius Annaeus Seneca

Important points to remember

- It is God who puts the different passions, gifts, and abilities in us.
- These passions, gifts, and abilities are what make us different from each other.
- Knowing our passions, gifts, and abilities leads us to live a focused life.
- Knowing your passions, gifts, and abilities makes you feel of value.
- Our passions give us reason to wake up in the morning.
- Our passions enable us to withstand challenges, because we have something to look forward to.
- Knowing our passions helps us to make good choices and focus our time on doing things that will help us to realise our passions.
- *Not knowing your passion makes life boring.*

Section 2

Created for a unique purpose

Preliminary notes to the facilitator

As believers and followers of Jesus Christ, each one of us is created to fulfil an assignment which contributes to the bigger purpose of God's creation. For God's kingdom to reign here on earth, He needs people to use—and we are the people God has chosen to use. If there are things in the society that we think do not make God happy, we have the responsibility as followers of Jesus Christ to correct those things. It is therefore very important that we ensure our young people understand this truth as early as possible.

In this section, the young people will be able to acknowledge their differences and not seek to be like others. This section is designed to help them love who they are and desire to become the best. It also seeks to lead the young people start visualising their abilities, passions, gifts, and talents as a solution to a particular challenge within society.

Learning objectives

- ❖ Identify the unique attribute (gift, talent, passion, ability) in their lives.
- ❖ Identify an area or issue within society that does not please them.
- ❖ Relate their unique attribute to the solution for the area or issue they are not pleased with.

2.1 What am I *currently* pursuing?

Learning outcome

By the end of this session, the young people will be able to relate *what* they are currently involved in with *how* they decided to take that path.

Materials required

- ❖ individual task 1 sheets
- ❖ printed handouts—important points to remember

Instructions to the facilitator(s)

- ❖ Give each young person in the class a copy of individual task sheet 1.
- ❖ Ask every young person to work by themselves without consulting anyone.
- ❖ Ask each one to keep their work for further reference.
- ❖ The class can discuss the questions generally.
- ❖ Conclude the topic by explaining the important points to remember allowing the young people to ask questions
- ❖ Give every young person a copy of the important points to remember

Individual task sheet 1

Please answer the following questions with sincerity:

➢ As a student, what are you studying to become?
➢ How did you arrive at the choice of your course?
➢ If you are not a student, what are you currently involved in, and how did you arrive at that choice?

Important points to remember

- It is very important to first know what you want to become in life.
- Knowing what you want to become will help you to choose the right career path.
- What you decide to study today needs to be something that will help you to fulfil your passion, gift, and/or talent.
- Following a career path that you are not passionate about will make the journey very tough, as there will be no motivation, especially when you start facing challenges.
- Some adults are not very happy with what they are doing because they did not choose by themselves what they wanted to become.
- Such people feel like they are living the dream of other people, which may include:
  - parents or guardians
  - cultural or social expectations
  - peers, who may exert pressure on others to behave in a certain way

- It is very important in life that you live out your own original purpose rather than an imposed one.

Table 2.1 **The difference between imposed and original life purpose**

Original life purpose	Imposed life purpose
It is *yours*.	It is *someone else's*.
It is about *your passion*.	It is about *someone else's passion*.
It helps to *please God alone*.	It is about *pleasing others*.

2.2   What do I want to become and achieve in life?

Learning outcome

By the end of this session, the young people will be able to identify their passion and the area(s) that they want to see change in society.

Materials required

- ❖ Individual task sheet 2
- ❖ Holy Bible
- ❖ printed handouts—important points to remember

Instructions to the facilitator(s)

- ❖ Give each young person in the class a copy of individual task sheet 2.
- ❖ Ask every young person to work by themselves without consulting anyone.
- ❖ Ask each one to keep their work for further reference.
- ❖ The class can discuss the questions generally.
- ❖ After the discussion, ask the young people to write on their individual task sheet 2 the scripture Ephesians 2:10.
- ❖ Conclude the topic by explaining the important points to remember allowing the young people to ask questions
- ❖ Give every young person a copy of the important points to remember

Individual task sheet 2

Please answer the following questions with sincerity. (Write your answers on a clean page, as you will use them later.)

- ❖ What makes you happy?
- ❖ Who inspires you the most? Why?
- ❖ What are you naturally good at?
- ❖ If you were to become the president or prime minister of a nation, what would you like to change? Why?
- ❖ Looking at the community, what makes you feel sad? Why?
- ❖ Whom do you feel needs more help in your community? Why?

Scripture to write on the task sheet

We are His workmanship, created in Christ Jesus for good works, which God prepared beforehand that we should walk in them.

Ephesians 2:10 NKJV

Important points to remember

- The things that we are good at, our passions, gifts, talents, and abilities, are normally meant to assist us in addressing the things in our community that make us sad.
- Each one of us has been given the ability to see something that is not good in society
- The things that make you unhappy, might not be the same to what makes somebody else unhappy.
- Most of the time if you are always unhappy about a situation around you, it could be a sign that God wants you to do something about it – change the situation!
- There are also different groups of people for whom you will always feel sorry for more than others.
- This could be a sign that God wants us to do something to change the lives of those people to be better.
- Being happy in life comes by making someone else's life better, which also makes life interesting.

Section 3

Vision and its importance

Preliminary notes to the facilitator

In life, when we do not know where we are heading, every wind that blows will be the one to lead us somewhere. Living a life without a vision will lead a person to go round and round in circles, until eventually the person realises he or she hasn't gone anywhere at all. A lot of time is wasted in people's lives because they are not sure of what they want to achieve with their lives.

When Jesus was about to leave the earth, He shared to His disciples the vision of every believer, saying, "Go therefore and *make disciples* of all the nations, baptizing them in the name of the Father and of the Son and of the Holy Spirit, *teaching them to observe all things that I have commanded you*; and lo, I am with you always, even to the end of the age. Amen" (Matthew 28:19–20 NKJV, emphasis added).

It is not enough for us to wish that people would commit their lives to Jesus. Instead, Jesus expects us to disciple other people, teach them to live the way He has taught us. It is through this the kingdom culture and lifestyle is established here on earth (cf. "Your kingdom come, Your will be done, on earth as it is in heaven").

As believers and followers of Jesus Christ, each one of us is created to fulfil an assignment which contributes to the bigger purpose of God's creation, His kingdom reigning here on earth. For God's kingdom to reign here on earth, He needs people —and we are the people for the assignment.

If there are things in society that we think do not make God happy, it is our responsibility as followers of Jesus Christ to correct those things. Inside our hearts, there will be *something* that will provide a solution for that challenge; that *something* in our hearts is what I consider a vision. It is therefore very important that we lead our young people to understand this truth as early as possible, so that they will always know that they do not merely exist, but live for a particular purpose.

Learning objective

❖ Understand what a vision is and why is it important in our lives as believers of Jesus Christ.

3.1   What is vision?

Learning outcome

By the end of this session, the young people will understanding the meaning of *vision* as it applies to their personal lives.

Materials required

- ❖ flip chart
- ❖ marker pens
- ❖ printed copy of Table 3.1 Types of people
- ❖ printed handouts—important points to remember

Instructions to the facilitator(s)

- ❖ Conduct an open discussion about what the young people think a vision is.
- ❖ Allow the young people to elaborate their answers.
- ❖ Write down on the flip chart the key points that the young people point out in their definitions.
- ❖ Discuss table 3.1 Types of people with the young people
- ❖ Conclude the topic by explaining the important points to remember allowing the young people to ask questions
- ❖ Give every young person a copy of the important points to remember

Table 3.1 **Types of people**

Types of people	
Those who are unaware of what is happening	Those who have no vision and who cannot see anything happening
Those who ask, "What has just happened?"	Those who have no vision but can see things happening
Those who make things happen	Those who have a vision and work to bring it into reality

Which type of person do you prefer from those described in Table 3.1?

Important points to remember

- Nothing that we see today was done without an initial vision.
- The houses we live in, the clothes we wear, the cars we drive on, the chairs we sit on, the books we read, the movies we watch, the music we listen to, and many other things we see are somebody's vision.
- What we see today, someone else saw in their mind and heart before it became reality.
- Vision is the ability to think about and plan for the future with a picture of the desired outcome.
- A vision is one of the greatest gifts a person can receive from God, because it is God's way of making us unique, different from other people.

3.2 The importance of having a vision

Learning outcome

By the end of this session, the young people will be able to understand the importance of having a vision for their lives.

Materials required

- ❖ Holy Bible
- ❖ flip charts
- ❖ marker pens
- ❖ printed handouts—important points to remember

Instructions to the facilitator(s)

- ❖ Divide the young people into groups of no more than four.
- ❖ Provide each group with a flip chart and a marker pen.
- ❖ Ask each group to write down four things they think will happen to a person who does not know what he or she wants to do or become in life.
- ❖ Let each group present their points, and allow time for discussion.
- ❖ Have the young people open their Bibles and read the scripture Proverbs 29:18a.
- ❖ Allow some time for discussion of that scripture, discovering what it means to the young people.
- ❖ Conclude the topic by explaining the important points to remember allowing the young people to ask questions
- ❖ Give every young person a copy of the important points to remember

Scripture reading

> Where the is no vision, the people perish.
>
> Proverbs 29:18a KJV

Important points to remember

- The poorest person is the one who lacks a dream to live for, a vision.
- Without a vision, it is not easy to know what you are aiming for. Not knowing where you are going will get you nowhere.
- Vision makes life very interesting. The continual dreading of Mondays and the continual looking forward to Fridays could be a sign that someone lacks vision, that he or she lacks motivation for life.
- Our individual vision distinguishes us from every other person.
- Vision gives our lives something to be focused on.
- It is through vision that we are able to transform the lives of people and the society we live in.
- Having a life vision keeps us focused and helps us to be free from distractions such as alcohol, drugs, and premarital sexual relationships.

3.3   What happens when we do not know our vision

Learning outcome

By the end of this section, the young people will understand how dangerous it can be when people do not have a vision. The impact is not only on the person without a vision but also on the lives of others and the world at large.

Materials required

- ❖ Holy Bible
- ❖ printed handouts—important points to remember

Instructions to the facilitator(s)

- ❖ Ask one young person to read Proverbs 29:18a.
- ❖ Conclude the topic by explaining the important points to remember allowing the young people to ask questions.
- ❖ Relate the important points to remember to the scripture read
- ❖ Give every young person a copy of the important points to remember

Scripture reading

> Where the is no vision, the people perish.
>
> Proverbs 29:18a KJV

Important points to remember

- Not having a vision makes life a cycle of trial and error.
- Not having a vision can lead to unprofitable connections, that is getting connected to the wrong people.
- Not having a vision makes it very hard to choose your major subjects in school.
- Not having a vision makes life meaningless and boring; there is no motivation to get up in the morning.
- The greatest consequence of not having a vision for our lives is the fact that those who were meant to benefit from our vision will be left in the dark.

Section 4

Who am I? My vision statement

Preliminary notes to the facilitator

God created each one of us in His image and likeness. With His image, we are able to live out God's character, and with His likeness, we have the ability to function like Him. As disciples of Jesus Christ, our main purpose for living is to ensure that God's kingdom comes to earth and that His will is done here on earth. This means that we are called to transform the way of life here on earth so that it reflects God's standards. In summary, God is *love*, and He wants this world to be a place where true love is demonstrated.

If we love God, we will work very hard to make sure that His love is experienced by every person we come in contact with. We will be able to achieve this if we identify an area we want to use to showcase this love. It can be music or entertainment, sports, business or economy, education, family, politics, or religion/faith.

Our young people need to understand this truth as early as possible so that they live a purposeful life, driven by God's desire to transform the people and the world He created into His image and likeness.

Our young people need to understand that as individuals, they are responsible for something that God wants them to address, and that He has put in them either a passion, a gift/talent, or a burning desire to see change. They need to bring out this gift and use in such a way that they are constantly reminded why they are here on earth.

God's Word says in Habakkuk 2:2–3 (NKJV), "Then the Lord answered me and said: '*Write the vision and make it plain on tablets*, that he may run who reads it. For the vision is yet for an appointed time; But at the end it will speak, and it will not lie. Though it tarries, wait for it; Because it will surely come, It will not tarry.'"

To be able to accomplish the tasks discussed in this section, you must have a ratio of one facilitator to four young people so as to enable closer supervision of the young people. Should the class be much bigger, it is better for the group to be divided into smaller sections.

Learning objectives

- ❖ By the end of this session, the young people will have their individual vision statements written.

4.1 Writing down my vision statement

Part 1

Materials required

- ❖ **Holy Bible**

- ❖ **Printed handouts—important points to remember**

Example of Vision Statement

(please enclose in one big text box starting from 'a bully-free... down to ...no bullying)

"A bully-free environment in England schools"

- – **What** – bullying problem

- – **Whom do you want to help** – students in England

- – **What result** – school with no bullying

Instructions to facilitator(s)

- ❖ Ask the young people to read Habakkuk 2:2–3 from the Bible.
- ❖ After the scripture has been read, ask the group to discuss what that scripture means to them.
- ❖ Use the example of vision provided to explain to the young people the three points that need to appear on a vision statement
- ❖ Conclude the topic by explaining the important points to remember allowing the young people to ask questions.
- ❖ Give every young person a copy of the important points to remember

Scripture reading

> Write the vision and make it plain on tablets, that he may run who reads it. For the vision is yet for an appointed time. But in the end it will speak, and it will not lie. Though it tarries, wait for it; because it will surely come, it will not tarry.
>
> Habakkuk 2:2–3 NKJV

Important points to remember

- What God has put in our hearts is also in His heart.
- When God put it in our hearts a desire to do something, He has already seen the outcome He wants.
- If we do not write down what we want to achieve with our lives, it will not be easy for us to always remember what we are doing; this can make us miss a lot of opportunities.
- Your vision statement will reflect your passion and will be something you are willing to do without worry of being paid or not.
- Your vision needs to be something that you will be able to do anywhere in the world. It is something you carry in your heart.
- Your vision must be rooted in love and not in fear, and its purpose must not be to seek praise from people.
- Your personal vision statement should include the answers to the following questions:
  - What do you want to do?
  - Whom do you want to help?
  - What result do you expect, and what value will you create or add?

Part 2

Materials required

❖ Individual task sheet 3
❖ white A4 paper

Instructions to the facilitator(s)

❖ Explain to the young people that the following exercise is going to be purely individual.
❖ It is an opportunity for them to bring out their uniqueness.
❖ Caution the young people not to compare themselves with anyone else, and emphasise the truth that they are all unique in whatever they desire to do.
❖ Emphasise that what makes us different is first knowing our purpose (vision) and then putting forth the effort to realise the vision.
❖ Distribute task sheets, explaining what needs to be done.
❖ Elaborate each point as indicated on the task sheet.
❖ After your elaborations, give each young person is a clean sheet of white A4 paper.
❖ Ask each young person to start the task by answering the four questions on the task sheet, writing their answers on the white A4 paper.
❖ Once the individual tasks are completed, begin a discussion.

Individual task sheet 3

Individual task

➢ For "What do you want to do?", start jotting down some action words, such as *educate, empower, encourage, give, guide, help, improve, inspire, motivate, nurture, organise, produce, promote, share, spread, teach, understand*, and *write*. These words will give you a picture of the actual task you will be involved in.

➢ For "Whom do you want to help?", start noting the different *categories that your task will target*; these will be your first group of contact, the ones you will carry out your assignment on. This group can be an organisation, a certain group of people (youth, the elderly, single men or women, teen mothers or fathers, widows, children, people with disabilities), animals, institutions (environment, media, business, faith bodies), etc. Identifying the different groups will enable you to start narrowing down the direct beneficiaries of your assignment.

➢ For "What result do you expect, and what value will you create or add?", start jotting down what you think would be the *outcome* of your intervention, and what possible *impact* it may have on your beneficiaries.

Part 3

Materials required

❖ Individual task sheet 4
❖ coloured A4 paper
❖ Holy Bible

Instructions to the facilitator(s)

❖ Go through the answers the young people have written on their sheets and discuss these with them in their smaller groups (of not more four).
❖ The aim of the discussions is to lead the young people to affirm that their answers describe something they are really passionate about.
❖ With all three questions answered, ask the young people to join their answers into one sentence.
❖ Go through the descriptions and edit them accordingly, without distorting the meaning.
❖ The resulting sentence ought to be the description of who they are and what they want to achieve with their lives.
❖ Ask the young people to read aloud what they have written about themselves to the rest of the group.
❖ As each of the young people reads their vision statement, affirm and emphasise to them the importance of embracing their uniqueness.
❖ Once all the young people have finished reading their statements, ask one young person to read John 14:12–14 NKJV.
❖ Now ask the young people to write their vision statements on the coloured A4 paper.
❖ They are to take the written vision statement home with them. Encourage them to hang it somewhere they will be constantly seeing it, to remind them of who they are.

Individual task sheet 4

> ➤ With all the points you have noted down, construct a sentence or two that captures the four bullet points.

Scripture reading

Most assuredly, I say to you, he who believes in Me, the works that I do he will do also; and greater works than these he will do, because I go to My Father. And whatever you ask in My name, that I will do, that the Father may be glorified in the Son. If you ask anything in My name, I will do it.

John 14:12–14 NKJV

4.2 Meeting with parents/guardians

Introduction

Many adults have grown to carry out the visions of those who raised them. Some parents/guardians have imposed what they think is better upon their children without providing room to hear out their children as they discuss their own passions and ambitions. This has resulted in many people who are not very pleased with their achievements. Inside, they carry a sense of unfulfilment, and the careers they have pursued have ended up as a burden to them.

This session is meant for the parents and/or guardians of the young people. The aim is to give them an understanding of how and why their children arrived at the place of writing down their vision statements.

With such an understanding, the parents or guardians will be able to support their children to become who God wants them to be. And even if the children feel they are called to something else later as they grow, they will still be able to apply the same principles and process to get to their life purpose.

Materials required

- ❖ Holy Bible
- ❖ written vision statements of the young people
- ❖ printed handouts—important points to remember

Instructions to the facilitator(s)

- ❖ Ask each young person to hold their vision statements in front of them and read it out loud.
- ❖ Ask the young people to read Isaiah 2:1–3, Habakkuk 2:2–3, and John 14:12–14 from the Bible.
- ❖ Conclude the topic by explaining the important points to remember allowing the parents and guardians to ask questions.
- ❖ Give every parent and guardian a copy of the important points to remember.

Scripture reading

> We are His workmanship, created in Christ Jesus for good works, *which God prepared beforehand that we should walk in them.*
>
> Ephesians 2:10 NKJV (emphasis added)

Important points to remember

- Every human being has a unique assignment, and an individual personality and traits/characteristics that are essential for their unique assignment.
- The assignment each individual has is to realise a profound solution to a specific challenge within society. We are God's workmen to carry out what He would do here on earth.
- The gifts, talents, and attributes that God has placed within us will be meaningful if they are used to meet the needs of others, not our own needs.
- Ideally God has called us to be full-time believers who represent Him in the pulpit, in the office, in the factory, in sports, or in our family—basically wherever we are and in whatever we do.
- Our children need to have this understanding. As young as they are, it will help shape their lives and determine the choices they make.
- As parents and guardians, we need to understand that when we draw our children away from their original purpose, they will begin living an empty life, which will eventually cause them to go astray—get involved in things that will not build them up.
- The difference between imposed and original life purpose is reflected in Table 4.1.

Table 4.1 The difference between an imposed and an original life purpose

Imposed	Original
• It is outward → inward.	• It is inward → outward.
• It reflects the needs of others and not the needs of the individual.	• It reflects the unique passion and individual traits of a person.
• It is rooted in fear and in seeking to please others.	• It is rooted in confidence and in seeking to please God and self.
• It provides temporary and fragmented satisfaction (there will always be a void in the inner self).	• It becomes the reason one desires to live another day to get up and continue pursuing one's purpose.
• Personal traits can sometimes contradict one's purpose.	• Purpose becomes an extension of the real individual.
• It is based on what other people think we are or what we should become.	• It is based on inner witness and is driven by love and passion.

Section 5

Setting my goals

Preliminary notes to the facilitator

Many people today live by way of chance. They have allowed the circumstances around them to determine the course their life takes. They do not have a plan of what they want to achieve because they are not sure of what tomorrow will bring.

> At any point in life, we are a result of a principle either applied or ignored.

Proverbs 21:5 reads, "*The plans of the diligent lead surely to plenty*, but those of everyone who is hasty, surely to poverty." This tells us that if we wish to succeed, we need to plan our lives. When we don't have a plan for what we want to achieve, we do things in haste, managing life crisis by crisis. Very little is achieved when there is no plan. This does not mean that our plans will be hundred per cent right, but they will provide us with guidance for achieving our passions and point out to us the areas of our lives which we need to improve. When we do not have goals, we have nothing to aim for. Having nothing to look forward to in life can become very dangerous, especially for a young person. In such a situation, the influence of peers can take a pre-eminent position. Getting involved with the wrong people can become very easy. Not only that, sinking into depression is another possible outcome.

Our young people need to start cultivating the habit of setting goals for themselves, as this will help them to avoid unnecessary distractions that might come on their way. We need to teach them that things in life do not just happen. They need to know that God has provided everything that we need to succeed in life; however, it is our responsibility to rise to the task and start making right choices and good decisions. We need to lead our young people to understand that the choices they make now will contribute to their quality of life in the future.

We also need to let them know that there is always room for amendment. Say they take the "wrong" steps early in their lives. As they continue to get closer to God, He opens their eyes, allowing them to see where they can make changes for the better. However, this must be a conscious decision-making process.

Learning objectives

By the end of this session:

- ❖ The young people will understand the importance of having goals in life.
- ❖ The young people will be able to set out their goals.

5.1   My overall goals

Part 1

Materials required

- ❖ Holy Bible
- ❖ printed handouts—important points to remember

Instructions to the facilitator(s)

- ❖ Ask the young people to read Psalm 90:12 from the Bible.
- ❖ After reading the scripture, the group is to discuss what that scripture means to them.
- ❖ Conclude the topic by explaining the important points to remember allowing the young people to ask questions
- ❖ Give every young person a copy of the important points to remember

Scripture reading

> So teach us to number our days that we may gain a heart of wisdom.
>
> Psalm 90:12 NKJV

Important points to remember

- A wise young person will start to become conscious of how they spend their time.
- One of the best ways to manage one's time is by having a set of goals to be achieved within a specified time frame.
- Our goals are a breakdown of our vision statement; they are the little things we do every day to become the best in life.
- God does not want anyone to waste time, because once it is gone, it is gone.
- Our goals need to be clear (specific) so that we can measure our progress.

Part 2

Materials required

- ❖ individual vision statements written on A4 paper
- ❖ Individual task sheet 5
- ❖ white A4 paper

Instructions to the facilitator(s)

- ❖ Given the importance of the exercise, enough facilitators are required so that each young person has one-on-one time with a facilitator. To make this happen, have a ratio of one facilitator to three young persons.
- ❖ Explain to the young people that the following exercise is going to be purely individual, as was the one when they wrote their vision statements.
- ❖ Explain to the young people that they will be writing down what they need to do to bring their vision to pass
- ❖ Each young person is to bring out their individual vision statement and read it out loud to remind themselves what they would like to become or achieve.
- ❖ Facilitator to distribute the task sheets.
- ❖ The young people are to be given enough time to work on the task. During this period, the facilitators should go around to each young person and guide them, as the task can appear to be daunting. *Every young person* must *have the attention of a facilitator during the exercise.*
- ❖ After a discussion between facilitator and individual young person, every young person to write their overall goals on a clean sheet of paper.

Individual task sheet 6

➤ Write down what you would like to realise in your lifetime; *these will be your lifetime goals.*
➤ These goals should be in line with your vision statement.
➤ Think freely about what the things are that you want to accomplish in different areas of your life (the facilitator should clarify this point).
➤ As young people, your education is a priority *now*, and therefore you need to start thinking what career path you want to pursue.

5.2 Where will I be in five years' time?

Introduction

It is important that we teach our young people to start thinking of their future. They can imagine the place they might want to be in the next five years. For example, someone who is 13 years old now knows that in five years' time they will be at university. What we want the young people to start thinking are things like which university will they like to go to, what they would like to study, what are the required grades for that course, what are the best subject combinations (while they are in secondary school), etc. Having these ideas in mind will help them to start working towards their goals.

Materials required

- ❖ individual overall goals sheets
- ❖ A4 sheets of paper
- ❖ Holy Bible

Instructions to the facilitator(s)

- ❖ Ask the young people to read Psalm 90:12 from the Bible.
- ❖ After the scripture is read, ask the group to discuss what that scripture means to them.
- ❖ Explain to the young people that the following exercise is going to be similar to the previous one they did to set their overall goals. The only difference is that the scope of the goals is narrower.
- ❖ Explain to the young people that the goals they are going to be writing down now are to be achieved in five years. That is, ask them to consider what they would like to be doing in five years.
- ❖ Distribute task sheets, explaining what needs to be done.
- ❖ Each young person should take out their Overall Goals sheet to remind themselves of their overall goals.
- ❖ Give the young people enough time to work on the task. During this period, the facilitators should go around to each young person and

guide them. *Every young person* must *have the attention of a facilitator during the exercise.*

❖ After a discussion between facilitator and individual young person, every young person to write their five-year plan on a clean sheet of paper.

Scripture reading

> So teach us to number our days that we may gain a heart of wisdom.
>
> Psalm 90:12 NKJV

Task sheet

> ## Individual task
>
> ➢ Write down where you see yourself in five years.
> ➢ This should be in line with your overall goals.

5.3 My focus for *now!*

Materials required

- ❖ individual five-year goals sheets
- ❖ A4 sheets of paper
- ❖ Holy Bible

Instructions to the facilitator(s)

- ❖ Ask the young people to read Psalm 90:12 from the Bible, reminding them of the lessons from the scripture.
- ❖ Explain to the young people that the goals they are going to write down now are to be *achieved within one year.*
- ❖ After explaining that, distribute task sheets indicating what needs to be done.
- ❖ Each young person should bring out their sheet of five-year goals to remind themselves.
- ❖ Distribute the task sheets and explain to the young people what is expected.
- ❖ The young people should be given enough time to work on the task. During this period, the facilitators should go around to each young person and guide them. *Every young person* must *have the attention of a facilitator during the exercise.*
- ❖ After a discussion between facilitator and individual young person, every young person to write their one-year goals on a clean sheet of paper.

Scripture reading

> So teach us to number our days that we may gain a heart of wisdom.
>
> Psalm 90:12 NKJV

Task sheet

Individual task sheet 7

➤ Write down where you see yourself in one year.
➤ This should be in line with your five-year goals.

5.4 Am I following my plan?

Materials required

- ❖ individual vision statements
- ❖ individual sheets listing overall, five-year, and one-year goals
- ❖ Holy Bible

Instructions to the facilitator(s)

- ❖ Ask the young people to read 1 Corinthians 10:12 from the Bible and to share with the group what the scripture means to them.
- ❖ Conclude the topic by explaining the important points to remember allowing the young people to ask questions
- ❖ Give every young person a copy of the important points to remember

Important points to remember

- When we set goals for ourselves, it is very important that we check on how we are progressing towards those goals.
- Checking how we are doing will help us to discover areas that we need to improve in. For example, if our goal was to earn an A in mathematics, if we get the A, we will be encouraged and motivated to maintain it or do even better. But if the results come and we have earned a C, we will have the opportunity to ask ourselves what went wrong, and we can then try to correct the problem.
- Constantly checking on ourselves can help us set new goals for ourselves.
- It is important that we check on ourselves regularly, depending on what it is we are aiming at. For example, there are things we can check on every week, and others that we can check on every month.
- If you think you cannot check on yourself, it is advised that you get somebody else to help you in that, someone who will be honest with you.

Scripture reading

So, if you think you are standing firm, be careful that you don't fall!

1 Corinthians 10:12 NIV

Section 6

I need to pray if I want to win

Preliminary notes to the facilitator

The majority of young people tend to think that prayer is something only adults and "mature" Christians do. They do not see themselves as can pray or as receiving answers to their prayers. *That is a big lie from the enemy, with the aim of keeping them off track!*

Prayer is a means God uses to establish and/or fulfil His Word. Our young people need to know that God has given us believers and followers of Jesus Christ the authority to determine what happens here on earth. This authority is exercised through prayer.

Some young people might have had the experience, or witnessed other people having the experience, of praying about something but the *expected/desired* answer has not yet arrived. To such young people, prayer can be something they find hard to accept. Our duty is to teach them the principles and purpose of prayer, so that any time they pray, they will pray with understanding.

Understanding the art of prayer makes our prayer life effective and fruitful. According to Dr Myles Munroe, prayer "has the power to transform lives, change circumstances, give peace and perseverance in the midst of trial, alter the course of nations and win the world for Christ. ... Prayer is an expression of mankind's unity and relationship of the love with God. It is an expression of mankind's affirmation and participation in God's purpose for the earth." Our young people need to know this truth!

> Prayer is a means of communicating with God to understand His purpose for creation and to know His heart!

Learning objectives

By the end of this session:

- ❖ The young people will understand the importance of prayer.
- ❖ The young people will understand how to pray using God's Word.

6.1   Why should we pray?

Materials required

- ❖ Holy Bible
- ❖ printed handouts—important points to remember

Instructions to the facilitator(s)

- ❖ Ask the young people to share with the group the main reason people should be praying.
- ❖ After the general discussion, ask two volunteers to read the Bible scriptures Luke 5:16, Luke 6:12, and Matthew 14:23.
- ❖ Conclude the topic by explaining the important points to remember allowing the young people to ask questions
- ❖ Give every young person a copy of the important points to remember

Scripture readings

So He Himself often withdrew into the wilderness and prayed.

Luke 5:16 NKJV

Now it came to pass in those days that He went out to the mountain to pray, and continued all night in prayer to God.

Luke 6:12 NKJV

And when He had sent the multitudes away, He went up on the mountain by Himself to pray. Now when evening came, He was alone there.

Matthew 14:23 NKJV

Important points to remember

- Our Lord Jesus Christ prayed!
- When we pray, we follow the example of our Lord Jesus.
- Prayer helps us to remain connected to God.
- Prayer is a way we talk to God.
- Prayer enables us to ask God to do His will here on earth.

6.2 Praying the right way

Materials required

❖ Holy Bible
❖ printed handouts—important points to remember

Instructions to the facilitator(s)

Part I

❖ Ask the young people to share with the group three main things they pray for.
❖ After the general discussion, ask one young person to read the Bible scripture Luke 11:1–4.
❖ Conclude part one of the topic by explaining the important points to remember allowing the young people to ask questions
❖ Give every young person a copy of the important points to remembe Part I

Part II

❖ Ask one young person to read the Bible scripture James 4:2b–3.
❖ Conclude part two of the topic by explaining the important points to remember allowing the young people to ask questions
❖ Give every young person a copy of the important points to remember Part II

Scripture reading 1

> Now it came to pass, as He was praying in a certain place, when He ceased, that one of His disciples said to Him, "Lord teach us to pray, as John also taught his disciples." So He said to them, "When you pray, say: Our Father in heaven, Hallowed be Your name. Your kingdom come. ^{Your will be done} on earth as it is in heaven. Give us day by day our daily bread. And forgive us our sins, for we also forgive everyone who is indebted to us. And do not lead us into temptation, but deliver us from the evil one."
>
> Luke 11:1–4 NKJV

Important points to remember Part I

- Our prayers show that we acknowledge God as being our Father and that we need His help.
- The *right prayer* is the one that asks for the fulfilment of God's will.
- Our prayers need to be related to our *vision* and *life goals*.
- Anything we ask God for that we need to help us fulfil our vision which is aligned to His will—for example, food, passing grades on our exams, protection—He will give us, to help us become better people.
- Before we pray, we must *ask God and other people for forgiveness* if we have done them wrong.
- Before God will forgive us, *we need to forgive others* who have done us wrong.

Scripture reading 2

> Yet you do not have because you do not ask. You ask and do not receive, because you ask amiss, that you may spend it on your pleasures.
>
> James 4:2b–3 NKJV

Important points to remember Part II

- When we ask God for things that will not help us to fulfil our vision, it is possible that our prayers will not be answered.
- When we do not pray, we hinder God's purpose from being achieved.

> The facilitator should let the young people know that there will be times when we will not be able to get each and everything exactly they way we wanted them. This is because God knows what is the best for us. Our job is to remain faithful.

Section 7

Managing my time

Preliminary notes to the facilitator

They say that time is money, but one of my teachers taught me that *time is life*! There are few things that all humans have been given in equal measure. One of those things is time. We are all given twenty-four hours a day. The richest human being on earth has only twenty-four hours a day, just the same as the poorest person. The difference in life is partly a result of what we choose to do with the twenty-four hours. There are three ways one can use one's time: either *spend it, waste it,* or *invest it*.

If we want our children to live their lives to the fullest, fulfilling their God-given purpose, we *must* enable them to understand their time and place. They must understand at what season they are in life and what the priority is during that season. Our young people need to understand that they do not have all the time in the world. They also need to understand that when they misuse and/or mismanage their time, it does not only affects their own lives, but also affects the lives of the people they are meant to impact/transform. We cannot afford to waste time. One truth about time is that *we can never recover the second that has just passed by.* As children of God, we desire to be good stewards of the resources God has placed on our hands, time being one of them!

Time is your most precious gift, because you only have a set amount of it.

—Rick Warren

Learning objectives

By the end of this session:

- ❖ The young people will understand the importance of time management to realising their passion/dream.
- ❖ The young people will start to develop strategies for ensuring that they manage their time well.

7.1   The importance of time management

Materials required

- ❖ Holy Bible
- ❖ printed handouts—important points to remember

Instructions to the facilitator(s)

- ❖ Ask for four volunteers from the group.
- ❖ Three of the volunteers will individually approach the remaining volunteer to invite him or her to an event.
  - ○ Event 1 is happening from 11:30 a.m. to 12:30 p.m.
  - ○ Event 2 is happening from 1:00 to 3:00 p.m.
  - ○ Event 3 is happening from 4:00 to 5:30 p.m.
- ❖ The approached volunteer is to decide which event he or she wants to attend.
- ❖ Remind him or her that there is the possibility of attending both events, as the time slots do not conflict.
- ❖ After the fourth volunteer takes a decision, ask him or her give the main reason for having taken the decision.
- ❖ Allow the other young people to share what decision they would have taken and why.
- ❖ After the general discussion, ask two volunteers to read the Bible scriptures Ephesian 5:15–17 and Colossians 4:5.
- ❖ Conclude part one of the topic by explaining the important points to remember allowing the young people to ask questions
- ❖ Give every young person a copy of the important points to remember

Scripture readings

> Be very careful, then, how you live—not as unwise but as wise, *making the most of every opportunity*, because the days are evil.
>
> Ephesians 5:15–16 *NIV* (emphasis added)
>
> Be wise in the way you act toward outsiders; *make the most of every opportunity.*
>
> Colossians 4:5 *NIV* (emphasis added)

Important points to remember

- God is the owner of time.
- In life, there are many things that will distract us.
- We should always ask ourselves what our priority is at any moment.
- Managing our time helps us to focus on what is important.
- If we manage our time, we will get more done in less time, and without struggling.
- Managing our time allows us to achieve what we desire.
- Recovering lost time is not an easy thing.

7.2 How do I manage my time?

Materials required

- ❖ flip chart
- ❖ marker pens
- ❖ printed handouts—important points to remember

Instructions to the facilitator(s)

- ❖ Ask the young people to sit in a circle.
- ❖ Ask each young person to say what time they get up during the school term and what they do before they go to school. Also ask them to say what time they finish school. Write their responses on a flip chart.
- ❖ Then, in turn, have each young person say one thing they do when they get home from school. The exercise is to continue until they feel they have shared everything they do after school, finishing with what time they go to bed. Write their responses on the flip chart.
- ❖ Again, in turn, have each young person say how they spend their day when they are not in school—such as at the weekends and/or on holidays—starting with the time they get up and finishing with the time they go to bed.
- ❖ From the points written on the flip chart, ask them which of those they *cannot live without doing* and why.
- ❖ The whole point of the exercise is to identify things that our young people might be spending their time on and to determine if those things are important or are robbing them of the time they could have used on other things that add value to their overall goals.
- ❖ Conclude part one of the topic by explaining the important points to remember allowing the young people to ask questions
- ❖ Give every young person a copy of the important points to remember.

Important points to remember

- Always plan your day and your week. Know what the things are that you want to get done. Since it is not easy to remember everything you want to do, write a list.
- Set the real times for when you want to do something.
- Block in time for your priorities, for example time to pray or time to study. During these times, do not allow anything to interfere. Allowing other things to interfere with your blocked-in time will cause your priorities to "melt away".
- If something very important comes up during your blocked-in time, make sure you compensate (e.g. by cutting out some of the free time you have allotted for yourself).
- Take *smart breaks*—which may consist of playing games, watching TV, or doing anything else that will refresh you.
- Learn to *say no* to things or people that will distract you from achieving your goals. Remember that *if you do not know how to manage your time well, other things and people will occupy it.*

There will be times when you will have to *give up* the things you like if you want to succeed in life. Such things might be:

- your phone or tablet
- your friends
- TV, and computer games or programs
- excessive sleep

- At the end of every week, take time to evaluate your goals and see if you are still on track to achieving them.

Section 8

General conclusion

> The greatest tragedy in life is not death, but a life without a purpose.
>
> People generally fall into one of three groups: the few who make things happen, the many who watch things happen, and the overwhelming majority who have no notion of what happens.
>
> —Dr Myles Munroe

Preliminary notes to the facilitator

It is essential that our young people grasp the importance of having something to pursue in life. That which we are pursuing in life must be something that will improve the lives of other people and also make the world a better place to live in.

Our young people need to understand that they are God's representatives here on earth. Jesus expects us to do the things He did and even more, just as it is written in John 14:12: "Most assuredly, I say to you, he who believes in Me, the works that I do he will do also; and greater works than these he will do, because I go to My Father."

This truth needs to be instilled into the minds of our young people so that they grow up knowing who they are. Our desire is to see our young people numbered among those who *make things happen* and not merely spectators.

Young people need to be reminded that even those people who are living on the streets, those who are drug addicts, those who are young offenders—some of them in prison—are people whom God created with a purpose. The reason some of them are in such situations is the fact that they never had an opportunity to be told and taught that they have a purpose here on earth. Others probable were taught but they chose not to follow the guidance they were provided with. *We do not want this to happen to our young people!*

8.1   Things I should never forget!

Materials required

- ❖ personalised printed A3 poster for every young person
- ❖ certificate of attendance for every young person
- ❖ light refreshments

Instructions to the facilitator(s)

- ❖ Prior the day of the session, liaise with the parents/guardians of the young people who successfully attended the entire course.
- ❖ Request a photograph of the children (preferably an electronic version).
- ❖ Get the vision statement of every young person.
- ❖ Paste the photograph and the vision statement on the poster template.
- ❖ On the last day, request the presence of the parents/guardians.
- ❖ Give the parents/guardians and the young people a summary of what was covered throughout the course.
- ❖ Explain to the young people the things they should always remember, and allow them to ask questions.
- ❖ Present each young person with a personalised printed poster
- ❖ Request that the parents/guardians of the young people step forward and stand behind their child (who will be holding their posters).
- ❖ Tell the parents/guardians that they have a role to play in helping their children realise their visions.
- ❖ Finally, present each young person with a certificate of attendance.
- ❖ Invite everyone to enjoy time together with some snacks prepared in honour of the young people.

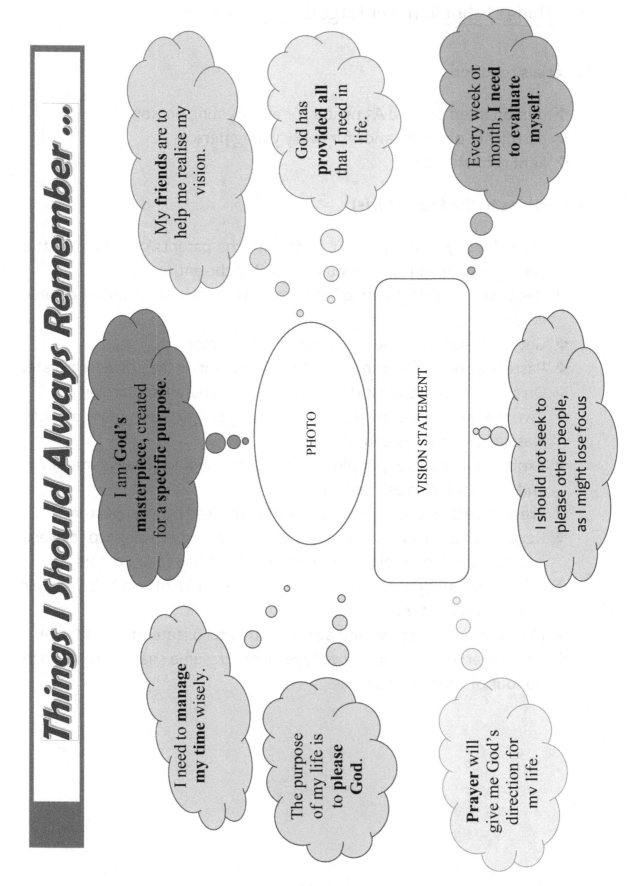

APPENDIX

QUESTIONNAIRE FOR PRELIMINARY SURVEY

1. What does it mean to be a Christian?

_____

_____

_____

2. Are you a born-again Christian? (Tick the answer applicable to you.)

Yes   No

3. Do you know people who are born-again Christians?

Yes   No

4. If you answered yes to question 2, do you remember praying the prayer of salvation?

Yes   No

5. If you are born again, what motivated you to become born again? (Tick the answer applicable to you.)

*   My parents are Christians.

*   My friend convinced me.

*   Somebody kept on preaching to me and I decided just to do it for his or her sake.

*   I sincerely wanted to do it.

*   Other reason. (Mention it.) _____

6. Do you pray?

6a)   Always

6b)   Sometimes

6c)   Not at all

7. If you chose option 6c, why do you not pray?

_____

_____

8. If you chose option 6a or 6b, what do you pray about?

_____

_____

9. Do you attend Sunday school or youth class in your church?

Yes   No

10. What topics do you like to be taught in Sunday school or youth class?

_____

Scenario 1 for Section 1.2

> There was a man who was well educated and who became an accountant. He secured a very good job with a very good bank in the country of Eden.
>
> His position provided him with the following privileges:
> - a free company house
> - a company vehicle with fuel provided
> - school fees for up to four children, up to the university level
> - a paid holiday of thirty working days per year.

Important points to remember for Section 1.2

❖ When God created humankind, all He saw was good.

❖ Every human being is created in the image and likeness of God.

❖ By image, it means we have the character of God in us. This means we are loving, caring, forgiving, faithful, respectful, etc.

❖ By likeness, it means we can function like Him. This means we have the nature to create things, and that we are organised, we keep time, we give our best to all we do, etc.

❖ Before God created humankind, He had made sure that all that human beings required to live a successful and fruitful life was provided for.

❖ God blessed human beings and gave them dominion over everything He had created, including all the animals. (It is amazing that in the beginning, human beings were not afraid of animals. Instead, they had authority over them.)

Scenario 2 for Section 1.3

His role exposed him to huge amounts of money. One time, he was tempted and stole £40,000, thinking nobody would know. Unfortunately, that very evening, the board of trustees conducted an unexpected audit and found out that there was some money missing. This man was dismissed immediately after the investigation.

Take time to discuss the following questions:
1. Why do you think the man stole the money?
2. Why did the board of trustees decide to dismiss him immediately, without considering the amount of experience and knowledge he had?
3. Who was affected by his dismissal? Explain why.

Important points to remember for Section 1.3

- When God put Adam in the garden, He told him not to eat of the fruit of the Tree of Life, saying that the day he would eat of it, he would surely die. We all know that Adam and Eve ate the fruit.
- When we disobey God, there are always consequences that follow.
- After Adam and Eve ate the fruit, God's glory left them and they discovered that they were naked. This also meant that the ability to rule over every creature on earth left them.
- From that time, human beings realised that they were naked. This meant that the glory of God had left them and they had therefore become exposed. They felt embarrassed/ashamed in front of each other.
- Sin disconnects us from God. If we are not connected to God, it is very easy for the Devil to attack us.
- God said to Adam, "Cursed is the ground for your sake."
- From that moment, the ground lost its glory and strange things started appearing on earth. The ground started growing thorns and thistles, things which had not been there in the beginning.
- Thorns and thistles are the things that make human life a struggle; up until today, they cause the life of humankind to be in bondage.
- Thorns can appear in different places; they can appear at the individual level, the family level, the societal level, or even the national level.
- In the world today, thorns appear in different forms, such as rebellion, anger, malice, jealousy, disrespect, corruption, prostitution, sexual immorality, family break-up, dishonesty, civil wars, crimes, relativism, and sicknesses/diseases. These and any other forms or manifestations of sin do not please God.

Scenario 3 for Section 1.4

Scenario 3

For the poor managing director, life was not as it used to be. First he was withdrawn from the Association of Accountants. Then he had to vacate the company house immediately. Next, his children were withdrawn from the private school they were attending because he could not afford the fees. Also, he had to start using public transport and sometimes walking to different places because he no longer had a company car. Life became unbearable.

Having been out of job for a while, he found that things became very tough. One day he thought to himself, *What if I write a letter of apology to the Association, express how deeply sorry I am, acknowledge my mistake, and outline to them how I propose to work on myself so that I will not fall into the same trap again?*

And indeed, this is what he did. The Association decided to give him a second chance. This time he had to ensure that he worked to the best of his ability. He even planned on educating other employees on the signs of temptation.

The man was back on track, and every day he constantly reminded himself that he was not immune to temptation. Having that constantly in his mind made him more alert to signs of temptation.

1. What was the *turning point* for the accountant?
2. Do you think the Association made the right decision in allowing him back to work? Why?
3. What do you think kept the man from falling into temptation again? Why?

Important points to remember for Section 1.4

- Sin always makes life hard.
- This is because God does not like to hang around where there is sin; and if God is not around, things are not good.
- For a very long time, people continued to sin, and they did not ask God for any forgiveness.
- This made them to continue to suffer.
- One time the children of Israel, thinking that they could no longer continue as they had been doing, *cried out to God*.
- God heard their cry and sent Moses to bring them out of oppression.
- Even in today's world, when we make mistakes, we can ask God for His forgiveness.
- God is forgiving and does not want any of us to suffer because of sin.
- When we ask Him for forgiveness, He is willing to forgive us. Once He forgives us, He makes us feel like we never sinned in the first place.

Important points to remember for Section 1.5.1

- At the right time God sent His Son Jesus to die for the salvation of all of humankind.
- Jesus carried all our sins.
- When He was hung on the cross, all our sins were hung there with Him.
- By accepting to die on the cross, He paid the price of sin on our behalf.
- For us to have the forgiveness of our sins, first we must repent of our sins; we must want to be forgiven.
- After we have been forgiven, we need to allow Jesus Christ to come into our lives. (Read John 3:3 again.)
- When He lives in us, He helps us to cease doing the wrong things.

Important points to remember for Section 1.5.2

- From the foregoing scripture, we see that God lost His friendship with Adam and Eve.
- Also, the ground was cursed and started to bring out thorns.
- God's losing His friends meant that Adam and Eve could no longer talk to God directly; they became very afraid of God and hid themselves.
- But because Jesus accepted to die on the cross for us, God regained His friends, and hope for a good life was given back to the earth.
- By the placing of the *crown of thorns* upon the head of Jesus, God's glory was restored on the earth. This means that we can overcome challenges through prayer.
- A reed is a sign of authority. When Jesus was *given the reed*, it meant that the authority that Adam and Eve lost to the satan in the garden was given back. So if we have Jesus in our hearts, we too have authority over sin and the things that God does not like
- When Jesus was *spat*, He was taking all the shame of our lives. Therefore, no one should ever make us feel that we are not of value.
- *Returning Jesus's clothes to Him* means that the original state of humanity was restored—the original Adam before he sinned.
- Because we have been saved by Jesus, He expects us to live like Him and to help other people come to know Him so that the world becomes the place which He created it to be.
- We can do this through the gifts, talents, and abilities He has given us.

Important points to remember for Section 1.5.3

- When we accept Jesus into our lives, all He wants from us is friendship. He wants us to be His friends.
- If we are His friends, we will always want to know what He wants.
- If we are His friends, we will always want to do what He wants.
- We will know what He wants by reading His Word.
- We will also know what He wants when we pray, because in prayer we receive good ideas which we did not have before.
- From His Word, we receive instructions on how to be good people and how not to sin against Him.
- If we notice that we have done something wrong, He wants us to repent straightaway.
- When we repent, we tell Him that we are sorry for what we have done and we request that He help us not to do it again.

Important points to remember for Section 1.6

- The reason we are believers in Jesus Christ is so that we can do His will here on earth.
- When we do the will of God here on earth, life becomes enjoyable.
- We will enjoy this life once we identify what we are very good at or passionate about.
- When we do the things we are good or passionate about, we have great joy within.
- However, life is normally not straightforward. There will be times when we will have to put in a lot of effort to get what we want.
- Some of the things we are good at or passionate about are used by other people in a very wrong or bad way, which does not please God. For example, there is music which is not good before God. There are some people who design clothes that are not very good. There are some leaders in the government who are not good. We see families are breaking up, we see people doing drugs, some people are homeless, and so forth.
- God has put in each one of us at least one thing we can do to make the wrong things right again; those things can be called areas of influence or areas of passion. For example, for people who are good or passionate about music, they can start producing good music which God likes. There might be people who would like to become leaders in the government. There might be those who are good at and passionate about fashion; they might design very beautiful and decent clothes. There may be people who do not want to see young people getting into drugs; other people who would like to feed the homeless; and people who do many other good things.
- Doing these good works might not be very smooth, but what will be pushing us to do them is the passion we have. But most importantly, we will do these things because we love God and we want to do what He asks us to do.
- We need to remember that if we do not do something about the problems of the world, those problems will start affecting us in one way or the other. For example, if we do not address the drug problem, then drug addicts might become thieves, stealing from other people. If someone does not work to help families, we might eventually see a lot of children

without parents. If someone does not write some good music to praise God, people will be listening to nothing but bad music.

- This means that each one of us needs to know what are we going to do to make this world a better place.

Question to think about:
What are you good at, or what are you passionate about, and why?

Important points to remember for Section 1.7.1

- Each one of has been given a specific ability, passion, or gift.
- God expects us to use that ability, passion, or gift to make Him known to others.
- If we are children of God and we use our gifts, passions, and abilities properly, many people will start to know what God wants for this world.
- When we go to church, we are taught God's truth about our lives so that we may become better people during the week when we are with people who are not of our faith.
- As we become better each day, we make God known, because people will always want to be like us. They will listen to us because they will see that we are giving them solutions to their problems.
- The sooner we discover our area of influence, the greater impact we will have in our community.
- Age is not a factor. Even young people have done great things to influence the world. (The facilitator can give practical examples of young people who are making an impact in their areas of influence.)

Important points to remember for Section 1.7.2

- It is God who puts the different passions, gifts, and abilities in us.
- These passions, gifts, and abilities are what make us different from each other.
- Knowing our passions, gifts, and abilities leads us to live a focused life.
- Knowing your passions, gifts, and abilities makes you feel of value.
- Our passions give us reason to wake up in the morning.
- Our passions enable us to withstand challenges, because we have something to look forward to.
- Knowing our passions helps us to make good choices and focus our time on doing things that will help us to realise our passions.
- *Not knowing your passion makes life boring.*

Individual task sheet 1 for Section 2.1

> **Please answer the following questions with sincerity:**
>
> ➢ As a student, what are you studying to become?
> ➢ How did you arrive at the choice of your course?
> ➢ If you are not a student, what are you currently involved in, and how did you arrive at that choice?

Important points to remember for Section 2.1

- It is very important to first know what you want to become in life.
- Knowing what you want to become will help you to choose the right career path.
- What you decide to study today needs to be something that will help you to fulfil your passion, gift, and/or talent.
- Following a career path that you are not passionate about will make the journey very tough, as there will be no motivation, especially when you start facing challenges.
- Some adults are not very happy with what they are doing because they did not choose by themselves what they wanted to become.
- Such people feel like they are living the dream of other people, which may include:
  - parents or guardians
  - those with certain cultural or social expectations
  - peers, who may exert pressure on others to behave in a certain way
- It is very important in life that you live out your own original purpose rather than an imposed one.

Table 2.1 **The difference between imposed and original life purpose**

Original life purpose	Imposed life purpose
It is *yours*.	It is *someone else's*.
It is about *your passion*.	It is about *someone else's passion*.
It helps to *please* God *alone*.	It is about *pleasing others*.

Individual task sheet 2 for Section 2.2

Please answer the following questions with sincerity. (Write your answers on a clean page, as you will use them later.)

➢ What makes you happy?
➢ Who inspires you the most? Why?
➢ What are you naturally good at?
➢ If you were to become the president or prime minister of a nation, what would you like to change? Why?
➢ Looking at the community, what makes you feel sad? Why?
➢ Whom do you feel needs more help in your community? Why?

Important points to remember for Section 2.2

- The things that we are good at, our passions, gifts, talents, and abilities, are normally meant to assist us in addressing the things in our community that make us sad.
- Each one of us has been given the ability to see something that is not good in society
- The things that make you unhappy, might not be the same to what makes somebody else unhappy.
- Most of the time if you are always unhappy about a situation around you, it could be a sign that God wants you to do something about it – change the situation!
- There are also different groups of people for whom you will always feel sorry for more than others.
- This could be a sign that God wants us to do something to change the lives of those people to be better.
- Being happy in life comes by making someone else's life better, which also makes life interesting.

Important points to remember for Section 3.1

- Nothing that we see today was done without an initial vision.
- The houses we live in, the clothes we wear, the cars we drive on, the chairs we sit on, the books we read, the movies we watch, the music we listen to, and many other things we see are somebody's vision.
- What we see today, someone else saw in their mind and heart before it became reality.
- Vision is the ability to think about and plan for the future with a picture of the desired outcome.
- A vision is one of the greatest gifts a person can receive from God, because it is God's way of making us unique, different from other people.

Table 3.1 **Types of people**

Types of people	
Those who are unaware of what is happening	Those who have no vision and who cannot see anything happening
Those who ask, "What has just happened?"	Those who have no vision but can see things happening
Those who make things happen	Those who have a vision and work to bring it into reality

Which type of person do you prefer from those described in Table 3.1?

Important points to remember for Section 3.2

- The poorest person is the one who lacks a dream to live for, a vision.
- Without a vision, it is not easy to know what you are aiming for. Not knowing where you are going will get you nowhere.
- Vision makes life very interesting. The continual dreading of Mondays and the continual looking forward to Fridays could be a sign that someone lacks vision, that he or she lacks motivation for life.
- Our individual vision distinguishes us from every other person.
- Vision gives our lives something to be focused on.
- It is through vision that we are able to transform the lives of people and the society we live in.
- Having a life vision keeps us focused and helps us to be free from distractions such as alcohol, drugs, and premarital sexual relationships.

Important points to remember for Section 3.3

- Not having a vision makes life a cycle of trial and error.
- Not having a vision can lead to unprofitable connections, that is getting connected to the wrong people.
- Not having a vision makes it very hard to choose your major subjects in school.
- Not having a vision makes life meaningless and boring; there is no motivation to get up in the morning.
- The greatest consequence of not having a vision for our lives is the fact that those who were meant to benefit from our vision will be left in the dark.

Important points to remember for Section 4.1 Part 1

- What God has put in our hearts is also in His heart.
- When God put it in our hearts a desire to do something, He has already seen the outcome He wants.
- If we do not write down what we want to achieve with our lives, it will not be easy for us to always remember what we are doing; this can make us miss a lot of opportunities.
- Your vision statement will reflect your passion and will be something you are willing to do without worry of being paid or not.
- Your vision needs to be something that you will be able to do anywhere in the world. It is something you carry in your heart.
- Your vision must be rooted in love and not in fear, and its purpose must not be to seek praise from people.
- Your personal mission statement should include the answers to the following questions:
  - *What* do you want to do?
  - *Whom* do you want to help?
  - What *result* do you expect, and what *value* will you create or add?

Individual task

➢ For "What do you want to do?", start jotting down some action words, such as *educate, empower, encourage, give, guide, help, improve, inspire, motivate, nurture, organise, produce, promote, share, spread, teach, understand,* and *write.* These words will give you a picture of the actual task you will be involved in.

➢ For "Whom do you want to help?", start noting the different *categories that your task will target;* these will be your first group of contact, the ones you will carry out your assignment on. This group can be an organisation, a certain group of people (youth, the elderly, single men or women, teen mothers or fathers, widows, children, people with disabilities), animals, institutions (environment, media, business, faith bodies), etc. Identifying the different groups will enable you to start narrowing down the direct beneficiaries of your assignment.

➢ For "What result do you expect, and what value will you create or add?", start jotting down what you think would be the *outcome* of your intervention, and what possible *impact* it may have on your beneficiaries.

Individual Task sheet 4 for Section 4.1 Part 3

> ➤ With all the points you have noted down, construct a sentence or two that captures the four bullet points.

Important points to remember for Section 4.2

- Every human being has a unique assignment, and an individual personality and traits/characteristics that are essential for their unique assignment.
- The assignment each individual has is to realise a profound solution to a specific challenge within society. We are God's workmen to carry out what He would do here on earth.
- The gifts, talents, and attributes that God has placed within us will be meaningful if they are used to meet the needs of others, not our own needs.
- Ideally God has called us to be full-time believers who represent Him in the pulpit, in the office, in the factory, in sports, or in our family—basically wherever we are and in whatever we do.
- Our children need to have this understanding. As young as they are, it will help shape their lives and determine the choices they make.
- As parents and guardians, we need to understand that when we draw our children away from their original purpose, they will begin living an empty life, which will eventually cause them to go astray—get involved in things that will not build them up.
- The difference between imposed and original life purpose is reflected in Table 41.

Table 4.1 **The difference between an imposed and an original life purpose**

Imposed	Original
• It is outward → inward.	• It is inward → outward.
• It reflects the needs of others and not the needs of the individual.	• It reflects the unique passion and individual traits of a person.
• It is rooted in fear and in seeking to please others.	• It is rooted in confidence and in seeking to please God and self.
• It provides temporary and fragmented satisfaction (there will always be a void in the inner self).	• It becomes the reason one desires to live another day to get up and continue pursuing one's purpose.
• Personal traits can sometimes contradict one's purpose.	• Purpose becomes an extension of the real individual.
• It is based on what other people think we are or what we should become.	• It is based on inner witness and is driven by love and passion.

Important points to remember for Section 5.1 Part 1

- A wise young person will start to become conscious of how they spend their time.
- One of the best ways to manage one's time is by having a set of goals to be achieved within a specified time frame.
- Our goals are a breakdown of our vision statement; they are the little things we do every day to become the best in life.
- God does not want anyone to waste time, because once it is gone, it is gone.
- Our goals need to be clear (specific) so that we can measure our progress.

Individual task sheet 5 for Section 5.1 Part 2

> ➤ Write down what you would like to realise in your lifetime; *these will be your lifetime goals.*
> ➤ These goals should be in line with your vision statement.
> ➤ Think freely about what the things are that you want to accomplish in different areas of your life (the facilitator should clarify this point).
> ➤ As young people, your education is a priority *now*, and therefore you need to start thinking what career path you want to pursue.

Individual task sheet 6 for Section 5.2

Individual task

➢ Write down where you see yourself in five years.
➢ This should be in line with your overall goals.

Individual task sheet 7 for Section 5.3

Individual task

➤ Write down where you see yourself in one year.
➤ This should be in line with your five-year goals.

Important points to remember for Section 5.4

- When we set goals for ourselves, it is very important that we check on how we are progressing towards those goals.
- Checking how we are doing will help us to discover areas that we need to improve in. For example, if our goal was to earn an A in mathematics, if we get the A, we will be encouraged and motivated to maintain it or do even better. But if the results come and we have earned a C, we will have the opportunity to ask ourselves what went wrong, and we can then try to correct the problem.
- Constantly checking on ourselves can help us set new goals for ourselves.
- It is important that we check on ourselves regularly, depending on what it is we are aiming at. For example, there are things we can check on every week, and others that we can check on every month.
- If you think you cannot check on yourself, it is advised that you get somebody else to help you in that, someone who will be honest with you.

Important points to remember for Section 6.1

- Our Lord Jesus Christ prayed!
- When we pray, we follow the example of our Lord Jesus.
- Prayer helps us to remain connected to God.
- Prayer is a way we talk to God.
- Prayer enables us to ask God to do His will here on earth.

Important points to remember for Section 6.2 Part I

- Our prayers show that we acknowledge God as being our Father and that we need His help.
- The *right prayer* is the one that asks for the fulfilment of God's will.
- Our prayers need to be related to our *vision* and *life goals*.
- Anything we ask God for that we need to help us fulfil our vision which is aligned to His will—for example, food, passing grades on our exams, protection—He will give us, to help us become better people.
- Before we pray, we must *ask God and other people for forgiveness* if we have done them wrong.
- Before God will forgive us, *we need to forgive others* who have done us wrong.

Important points to remember for Section 6.2 Part 2

- When we ask God for things that will not help us to fulfil our vision, it is possible that our prayers will not be answered.
- When we do not pray, we hinder God's purpose from being achieved.

Important points to remember for Section 7.1

- God is the owner of time.
- In life, there are many things that will distract us.
- We should always ask ourselves what our priority is at any moment.
- Managing our time helps us to focus on what is important.
- If we manage our time, we will get more done in less time, and without struggling.
- Managing our time allows us to achieve what we desire.
- Recovering lost time is not an easy thing.

Important points to remember for Section 7.2

- Always plan your day and your week. Know what the things are that you want to get done. Since it is not easy to remember everything you want to do, write a list.
- Set the real times for when you want to do something.
- Block in time for your priorities, for example time to pray or time to study. During these times, do not allow anything to interfere. Allowing other things to interfere with your blocked-in time will cause your priorities to "melt away".
- If something very important comes up during your blocked-in time, make sure you compensate (e.g. by cutting out some of the free time you have allotted for yourself).
- Take *smart breaks*—which may consist of playing games, watching TV, or doing anything else that will refresh you.
- Learn to *say no* to things or people that will distract you from achieving your goals. Remember that *if you do not know how to manage your time well, other things and people will occupy it.*

> There will be times when you will have to *give up* the things you like if you want to succeed in life. Such things might be:
> - your phone or tablet
> - your friends
> - TV, and computer games or programs
> - excessive sleep

- At the end of every week, take time to evaluate your goals and see if you are still on track to achieving them.

References

1. Adelaja, S (2009), Time is Life: History Makers Honor Time, Favor Publishing House
2. Cloud & Townsend, (1992), Boundaries: When to Say Yes, How to Say No To Take Control of Your Life, Zondervan
3. Munroe, M. (2002), Understanding the Purpose and Power of Prayer, Whitaker House
4. Munroe, M. (2003), Principles and Power of Vision, Whitaker House
5. Munroe, M. (2006), Kingdom Principles: Preparing for Kingdom Experience and Expansion, Destiny Image
6. Warren, R. (2002), The Purpose Driven Life: What on Earth am I Here for, Zondervan
7. http://quotationsbook.com/quote/17170/

The author would like to know what you think
about this training guide by sending your comments
to: rebuildingthewalls18@gmail.com

About the Author

June Clare Bugenyi is the co-founder of Personal Potential Discovery Program, a forum whose aim is to enable young people to establish their identity in Christ, identify their unique abilities, and pursue their purpose in life.

She desires to see people living a purposeful life, a life that is centred in transforming individuals, families, communities, and nations for the better.

June is a community and social development worker, with skills in project design, project planning and implementation, and project evaluation. She has skills in training design and facilitation, and volunteers with charitable organisations. June also likes to watch movies, sing, read books, cook, and bake.

Her life experience as a senior single lady, the firstborn of a single parent and the tragic event of losing her only parent, formed the basis for her passion to see people living a purposeful life. Without a purpose to pursue, life for June could have been a more painful journey!

Printed in the United States
By Bookmasters